The Presentation on Presentations

The 'Lazy' way to becoming a more confident public speaker from

Peter Taylor

THE PRESENTATION ON PRESENTATIONS

THE PRESENTATION ON PRESENTATIONS

Copyright © 2012 Author Name

All rights reserved.

DEDICATION

I would like to dedicate this book to Joyce and Brian Taylor, my Mum and Dad – love you both and thank you for everything

ACKNOWLEDGMENTS

I would like to thank every person who has ever booked me to speak, attended one of my presentations (if you enjoyed it then 'you're welcome' and if you didn't then 'I'm sorry'), and anyone who has suggested me as a possible speaker at an event – your support has been amazing over the last 10 years since 'The Lazy Project Manager' was published and I began my speaking journey. www.thelazyprojectmanager.com lists every one of the events, conferences, congresses, webinars and interviews from the very first one on 6th April 2009 - PMI North & Midlands Chapter meeting: 'PMO, a 3-year journey'.

And, of course, I look forward to many more opportunities to speak, meet and learn from others.

With 387 speaking events delivered to date then I think 500 would be a great personal target to aim for before I hang up my microphone; and besides, I still haven't made it to Iceland and so there remains that challenge.

That, of course, is a real hint to contact me soon.

1 THE AUTHOR

Peter Taylor is a PMO expert who has built and led four global PMOs across several industries and has advised many other organisations in PMO and Project Management strategy.

He is also the author of the number 1 bestselling project management book 'The Lazy Project Manager', along with many other books on project leadership, PMO development, project marketing, project challenges and executive sponsorship.

In the last 10 years, he has delivered over 380 lectures around the world in over 25 countries and has been described as 'perhaps the most entertaining and inspiring speaker in the project management world today'.

His mission is to teach as many people as possible that it is achievable to 'work smarter and not harder' and to still gain success in the battle of the work/life balance.

His other mission, in case you missed it earlier, is to actually get to visit Iceland.

More information can be found at www.thelazyprojectmanager.com – and through his free podcasts in iTunes.

THE PRESENTATION ON PRESENTATIONS

The above probably comes under the heading of 'blah, blah, blah' – see chapter: The Start.

Peter Taylor was born quite a long time ago, lives in Sandhurst in the United Kingdom, likes Red Bull, Wine Gums and reading crime thrillers such as those written by Jo Nesbo (often at the same time), is a Virgo in every sense, and listens to lots of music, but especially likes Black Sabbath.

He drives a red Audi A5, loves Clint Eastwood films and tries to support the England football team (which isn't always easy).

He is writer and speaker, and tries, very, very hard, to make people smile as much as possible whilst sharing some snippets of knowledge.

And he has travelled extensively but hasn't yet made it to Iceland.

The above probably comes under the heading of 'more interesting in some ways' – again see chapter: The Start.

2 THE SPEAKER

Am I a public speaking expert?

An interesting thought and hardly one that I could answer myself.

I could say, with complete accuracy, that I have (at the time of writing this book) delivered 337 presentations of varying formats to a public audience of varying human formats, interests, locations and languages (to over 60,000 people in actual fact). I could also say that I continue to get interest and bookings for future events.

I could say that I really enjoy the buzz of being on stage and the feeling of a job well done and presentation well delivered, whilst also trying to get better each time.

I could add, with some humility, that there are many kind words from people around the world who have enjoyed my presentations and aren't afraid to admit it in public (check out my LinkedIn profile).

But I can't say I am an expert.

I am continually amazed when I see other people present, the good ones that is, the skill and gift that they have in this form of communication, and I always try and learn from them and these experiences.

THE PRESENTATION ON PRESENTATIONS

But I was increasingly asked by people about public speaking. How did I start out? How do I manage to stand up on stage? What tips and techniques I can offer? That sort of thing.

And so I challenged myself to put together a presentation on, well on presentations.

The 'Presentation on Presentations' is my second most popular topic (after 'The Lazy Project Manager') and the abstract goes like this: We aren't born to be professional level presenters but through this entertaining presentation the 'rights' and 'wrongs' of good presentations are explored along with a 'how to prepare' for that all-important event. With a few simple lessons taught through the very medium of 'presentation' the audience will take away some great ideas for improving their own technique and 'death by PowerPoint' is definitely not the outcome.

After a few deliveries of this I started making some notes to share with my audiences and this evolved into a rough simple guide. It also evolved in to a one day 'Presentation Skills' workshop – see the end of this book.

And now, I have decided to take that simple guide and add some more words and experience notes and make it into a book.

A short book you will note, after all, the essence of all my work is that 'less is more' and really you don't need to read an 80,000 word epic tome when all you are actually doing is trying to present a message, of some form, in an effective, simple and efficient way.

Therefore, this is a more a reference guide with 'simple to adopt tips and techniques' on the main points of good presentation.

3 THE PROLOGUE

I was recently in a restaurant in a foreign land (well foreign to me of course but less so to the locals).

The location was good, the décor and ambience very acceptable, the company most enjoyable, and the snow fell softly outside providing a winter wonderland visual delight through the large windows.

But sadly, all of that positive build-up for a great evening's dining was almost outweighed by the food and service.

After an initial ordering experience the diners elected to eat the same main course but each agreed that the chef's vegetable of choice for the evening was not to their personal liking. It was the humble Brussels sprout, a member of the brassica family that enjoys a somewhat tarnished image which, considering its status as a nutritional powerhouse, is a little unfair. Its reputation is perhaps mostly due to the great British Christmas Day cooking technique: take sprouts, cut, trim, boil until at least twice dead and then for five minutes more. Then, finally, pile into a large dish and leave – because nobody actually likes Brussels sprouts (at least not cooked this way).

Anyway, the request was made to replace said evil vegetable with an alternative, and asparagus tips were requested. And so the meal continued through a mediocre appetizer and on until the main course finally arrived … without Brussels sprouts (the good news) but also without anything in their place, such as the asparagus tips, as requested (the bad news).

The waiter was recalled and cajoled and encouraged to resolve this rapidly, at which the staff applied all of their skills and training, by ignoring us and disappearing. Eventually after a long period, during which most of the meal was consumed, the waiter did reappear and proceeded to almost, but not quite, save the entire situation.

With a silver platter and a silver fork of delicate proportions the waiter proceeded to ceremoniously, and with great flourish, place two small asparagus tips across the centre of each diner's remaining half-eaten meal.

It was theatrical and exaggerated and, had it not been for the sheer humour of the whole thing, he may just have got away with it.

Presentation can win the day.

There is an old story about a crisis in a company when it was discovered that one of their products was actually killing customers. This was a major issue and one that delivered headlines that were very bad news for the company.

However, a savvy and spirited marketing executive quickly went to work to resolve the situation. After a few days of bad publicity and press, with the death toll mounting, the marketeer launched a major fight back.

The first press release read 'Company X extremely concerned for its customers…'

Sadly, the problems continued, and more customers met their maker as a result of the killer products. The bad publicity continued, and the situation looked desperate.

The marketing executive did not walk away from the challenge nor did she give up the battle. She worked late into the night thinking

THE PRESENTATION ON PRESENTATIONS

blue sky thoughts about a solution to this issue and finally came up with a plan.

The next day a press release was delivered to the world at large that simply read 'Company X sees a massive reduction in dissatisfied customers…'

It is all in the presentation and in turning negatives in to positives.

Our waiter tried but just failed; he couldn't carry it off completely and is probably from Barcelona anyway (yes that is a Fawlty Towers reference and not an insult to wonderful Barcelona, one of my favorite cities).

Presentation counts. So, make it count for you, and I hope this small book helps in some way.

4 THE START

The above quote is real – and this is (not) my Mother – and the two are (not) connected!

But it does deliver a great introduction to a presentation and helps relax the audience and get them to believe that this will be an enjoyable experience, or at least give me the benefit of the doubt for now.

The most important thing is to start in a way that you feel comfortable with and that is also appropriate to the audience and presentation purpose.

You can, as above, start with something amusing and attention grabbing.

Surprise your audience.

Or you can gently ease your way into the presentation.

But don't go for the big joke or anything risky, this is also about you starting confidently and without stress – so use proven material you know well.

And by 'gently easing' I certainly do not mean mumble your way into a state of boredom inducing dullness.

Just think about the start as it is a very important point in your presentation. Just drifting into your time with your audience is not what you want to do. You really want to impress and impact. And if you don't then why are you bothering at all?

5 THE PRESENTER

You can certainly start with some formal introductions, especially if members of the audience do not know who you are or what you do – but keep it brief (very brief).

You can also have your (brief, very brief) bio read by someone else.

Both options work well as long as (have I mentioned this already?) that it is brief.

But remember this bit. It is really quite important. This will not really connect you with the audience – many, if not most, will just hear 'blah, blah, blah!'

THE PRESENTATION ON PRESENTATIONS

So how can you do something different that will actually engage your audience and keep them interested?

If you use a lot of personal (or work) information about you then each member of the audience is more likely to pick up on at least one thing that they can relate to – and therefore connect to.

In the above I talk about my family, my interests, my home, and my travels – all in a very short time but it really does engage an audience I have found – see Chapter 2: The author.

Also read James Kane – The Loyalty Switch – to find out more about this technique.

Of course, think about your audience, this type of introduction might not fit the occasion, but I feel there is always an opportunity to include something personal.

6 THE SANITY CHECK

> **How are we doing so far?**
>
> The 10 minute 'window'
>
> ✓ Competent
> ✓ Likeable
> ✓ Interesting
> ✓ Worth staying awake for?

OK, so you have begun well, and things are looking good for the rest of the presentation, as far as you are concerned that is, but what about your audience?

It is time to check in with your audience to ensure that they are still with you.

THE PRESENTATION ON PRESENTATIONS

Always check in with your audience, throughout your presentation. It is amazing how many speakers seem to almost forget the audience exists when they are in full flow.

You have about ten minutes into a presentation to keep or to lose an audience (we will come back to audiences shortly, some members you may never actually have, but most are at worst neutral at the very start).

The '10-minute window' is when you need to do two things:

- Breathe
- Think

Breathe, because, if you are nervous about this delivery then the most common thing that happens is that your heart is racing and your words follow at the same speed, and so now is an excellent time to stop and take a calming deep breath and relax a little. If you don't you will only get faster and faster and miss the opportunity to communicate well with your audience.

Think, because if you blindly go on and you have already lost most of your audience then again, you will miss the opportunity to communicate well with your audience.

I am not talking about taking a short tea break here but taking a sip of water and looking at your audience delivers both breathing and thinking time, and your audience won't know what you are actually doing.

And anyway, drinking throughout a presentation is a good thing (water of course, although see Chapter: The stories from the stage, there is a potential risk even with water).

7 THE FEAR OF PUBLIC SPEAKING

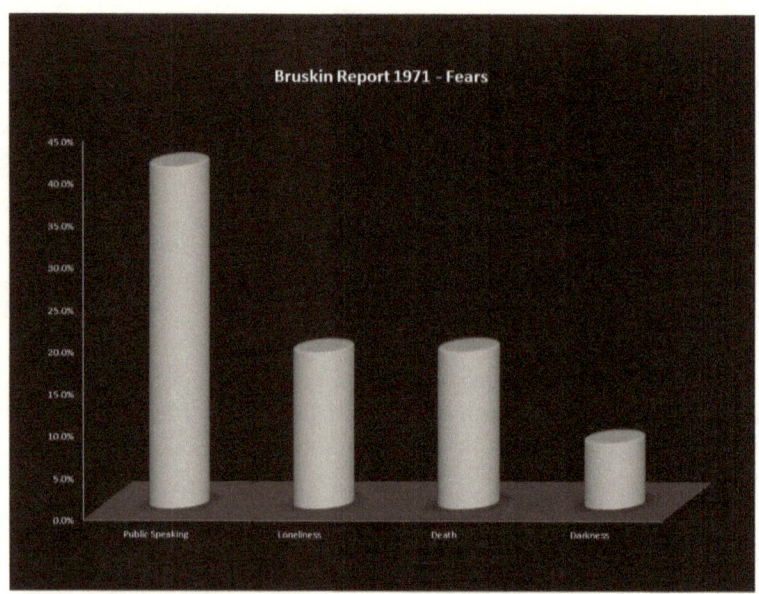

In 1971 the Bruskin Report was completed, conducted by the U.S. marketing research firm R. H. Bruskin Associates for the [American] Travel Research Association.

The people at Travel Research wanted help dealing with what they thought was a big marketing problem for the travel industry and

THE PRESENTATION ON PRESENTATIONS

that was the Americans fear of flying.

Bruskin was delighted to be able to help them out with their survey which somehow managed to show that ordinary Americans were much more afraid of public speaking, of heights, of insects, of financial problems, of deep water, and sickness, and even death than they were of flying.

There were, as you may suspect, many flaws with this piece of research but it does lead us to the point that we know only so well, that many people are downright terrified of speaking in public. Based on the above chart people, it seems, would rather die alone in the dark than speak in public.

But in the workplace, and perhaps to a lesser degree in our private lives, some form of public speaking on the rare occasion is rather hard to avoid.

Hence the 'Presentation on Presentations' and hence this book.

I want to help, if I can, and so read on to learn about your audience. In fact, it is the audience, or fear of, that could be why so many suffer from glossophobia.

Glossophobia or speech anxiety is the fear of public speaking. The word derives from Greek words meaning tongue and fear or dread.

8 THE AUDIENCE

Now here is the real challenge with audiences.

Try this out yourself, on yourself and on some friends or colleagues. Ask two questions:

- How many of you have been in the audience of a

THE PRESENTATION ON PRESENTATIONS

presentation?
- How many of you have been in the audience of a bad presentation?

Conclusion: Experts then!

That's the key here isn't it? – we all know what makes for a lousy presentation experience and therefore we know what makes for a good presentation experience and so every time you speak/present you are faced with a group of experts!

Experts who may or may not want to be there, experts who may or may not care about you or what you have to say, and experts who may or may not know that they are indeed experts. But they are experts anyway. They are potentially the toughest critics you may ever face in your life.

OK I realise at this point that I am supposed to be helping you and not making you even more nervous than you might already be, but you really do have to understand those that sit and face you in a presentation room.

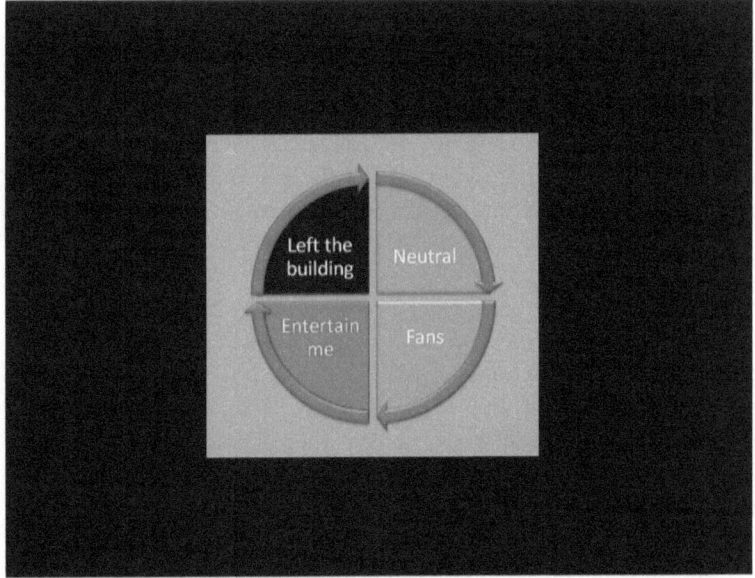

THE PRESENTATION ON PRESENTATIONS

What matters now is to actually understand your audience – they are the scary ones remember, the ones whose eyes burn deep into your soul with unbridled expertise as you look at them.

They will be made up of 4 (not always equal) groups:

1. The 'neutrals' – they are open to listening to you if you are worth listening to – at this point in the presentation you will have won or lost them (the ten minute rule) so that start is really important
2. The 'fans' – who have heard you before, work with you, are your closest colleagues and will love you regardless, nice to have a few of these for sure
3. The 'entertain me' ones – the people who are challenging you to prove they should have to listen to you – by this point the best you can hope is that they are still challenging you
4. The 'I've left the building' ones – this group are there in body but not in spirit and will resist any efforts to win them over – that may happen later on through peer pressure from all of your new fans of course but not during the presentation itself

Peers are potentially the worst – but they still fall in to these four groups.

If you can, assess your audience beforehand and think of what the mix will be. Then prepare yourself for the reality that Juliet might well sit in the front row staring at you with arms folded throughout the presentation, and just accept that is the way it will be.

Focus your energies and engagement on the others and who knows, Juliet might well come to accept that what you are saying makes sense. All things are possible.

Keep reading your audience to gauge interest and attention and, deviate from plan if you really need to, don't be afraid to go 'off piste' if things are really going badly as far as attention is concerned – stop, ask the question of the audience, what they are feeling at this point?

THE PRESENTATION ON PRESENTATIONS

And, whilst you do have to consider your complete audience, you will also do well to focus a little more attention on the key attendees, the decision makers, the authorities and those that advise the preceding list.

9 THE PURPOSE

Why are you presenting? I believe, in a work environment, that there are three major reasons:

1.   To convince
2.   To educate
3.   To prove

THE PRESENTATION ON PRESENTATIONS

There is a fourth reason which is more likely to be outside of work, but not always, and that is 'Occasion'. My daughter, for example, is living in fear of my 'father of the bride' speech – which is probably why she hasn't got married as yet!

With regards to the other three they all require a slightly different structure, but the main thing is to realise what it is you are trying to convey and design your presentation accordingly.

Trying to fit all three into to one 30-minute presentation is really not going to work.

Treating all presentations as the same is also going to weaken your delivery.

So, before you start cranking out those magnificent PowerPoint slides consider for a few moments exactly what it is you are trying to do.

10 THE CONTENT

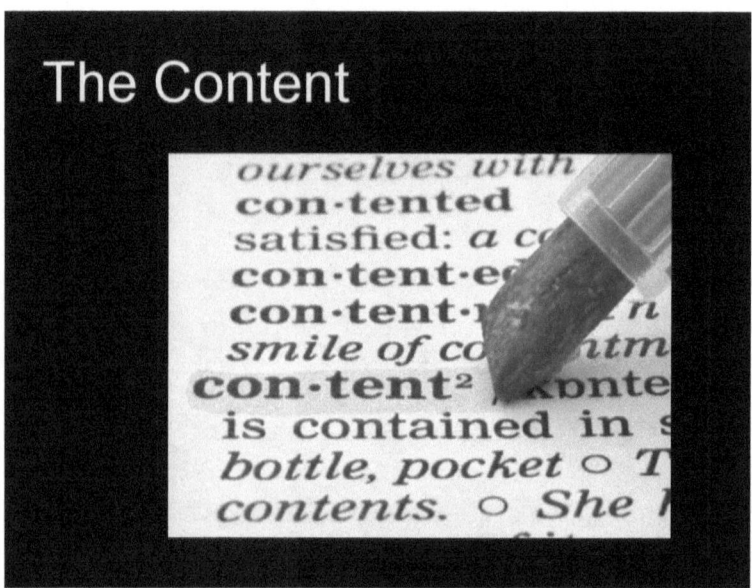

Having understood what it is that you are trying to achieve then now you can consider what you are presenting about.

If this is your 'pet' subject or expertise – then you know the details, but the risk is to get carried away – time yourself, control yourself, limit yourself even. Burning through all of your time and not reaching a point of achievement (convincing, educating or proving)

THE PRESENTATION ON PRESENTATIONS

will mean it has all been a waste of time. Perhaps an entertaining waste of time, but a waste of time, nonetheless.

If this is something you have been 'volunteered' for – you might not have all the detail – so do dry runs, get help, plant a supporter 'expert' in the audience in case you get stuck. Remember asking for clarification during a presentation is absolutely fine.

And don't try and deliver 100% in the presentation – takeaways/hand-outs/follow-ups are all acceptable (after the event – not handed out during or beforehand).

Crib notes are also more than fine – but think of ways to make these 'invisible' or simple at least. See Chapter: The crib notes.

11 THE TIME

The big pressure is time.

Think of time the right way round though.

THE PRESENTATION ON PRESENTATIONS

In my world the average presentation is 60 mins long – and let's say the average audience is 100 in number. Therefore 1 hour of my time is consumed (plus preparation time of course) but 100 hours of my audience's time is the true measure. That is 100 hours wasted if I am no good. That is 4.2 days! That's a lot!

Last year I presented to around 7,000 people, so 292 days of listening time!

It is better to prepare and deliver a great 30 minutes rather than a mediocre 60 minutes.

Hands up who has ever complained about a presentation finishing early. Precisely!

And be warned, as if you needed to be. Time is a very flexible beast.

You need to be prepared to adapt to time constraints – time of day – organiser's demands to reduce time (you never get offered more time) – overruns from earlier presenters – be flexible, be ready to adapt and not miss the opportunity.

And remember – less is most certainly more.

THE PRESENTATION ON PRESENTATIONS

19th Nov 1863 – The Gettysburg Address

The Gettysburg Address is a speech by U.S. President Abraham Lincoln that is one of the best-known speeches in American history.

It was delivered by Lincoln during the American Civil War at the dedication of the Soldiers' National Cemetery in Gettysburg, Pennsylvania four and a half months after the Union armies defeated those of the Confederacy at the Battle of Gettysburg.

An event that was actually planned and led by Edward Everett but his 2-hour 13,607-word oration is long forgotten –

whereas Abraham Lincoln's few minutes and 271 words isn't

… the rest is history…

> *Four score and seven years ago our fathers brought forth on this continent a new nation, conceived in liberty, and dedicated to the proposition that all men are created equal.*

THE PRESENTATION ON PRESENTATIONS

Now we are engaged in a great civil war, testing whether that nation, or any nation so conceived and so dedicated, can long endure. We are met on a great battlefield of that war. We have come to dedicate a portion of that field, as a final resting place for those who here gave their lives that that nation might live. It is altogether fitting and proper that we should do this.

But, in a larger sense, we can not dedicate, we can not consecrate, we can not hallow this ground. The brave men, living and dead, who struggled here, have consecrated it, far above our poor power to add or detract.

The world will little note, nor long remember what we say here, but it can never forget what they did here. It is for us the living, rather, to be dedicated here to the unfinished work which they who fought here have thus far so nobly advanced.

It is rather for us to be here dedicated to the great task remaining before us—that from these honoured dead we take increased devotion to that cause for which they gave the last full measure of devotion— that we here highly resolve that these dead shall not have died in vain—that this nation, under God, shall have a new birth of freedom—and that government of the people, by the people, for the people, shall not perish from the earth.

Perhaps one of the greatest examples of less being very, very much more.

12 THE TOOLS

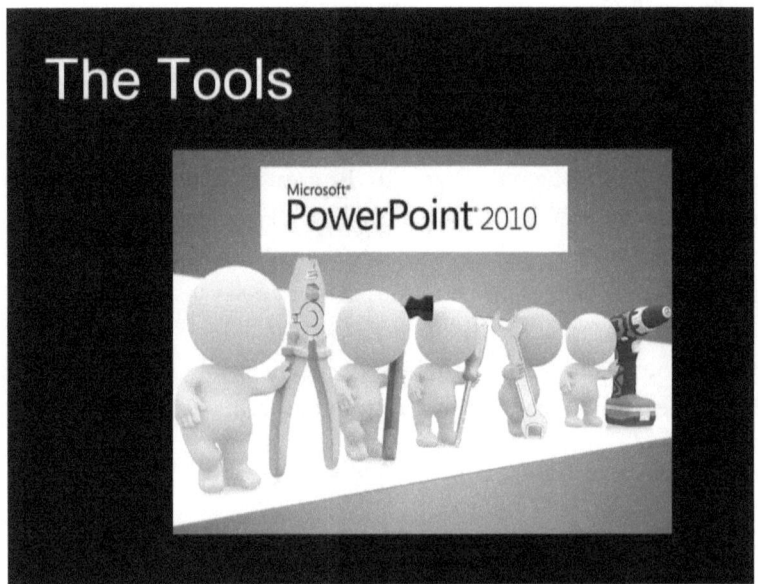

Let's start with the slides themselves, or indeed whatever format you are utilising for your presentation. There are two things to remember here:

- The slides are for your audience and not you!
- You should know your material (and not need the slides)

THE PRESENTATION ON PRESENTATIONS

So many people use the slides themselves as the reference material for their presentation, with the often-seen risk of the slides being so dense in text as to be unreadable (and also boring) for the audience. Which also leads to presenters 'reading their slides out loud' instead of actually presenting (once again boring in the extreme for any audience). People also create slides that are effectively the handouts for the session, which is a lazy way of presenting in my view as the two have very different purposes.

THE PRESENTATION ON PRESENTATIONS

13 THE FORMAT

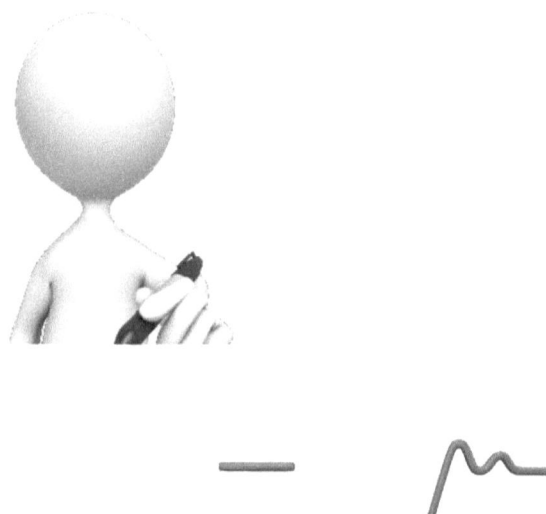

Many clever graphics can be incorporated into PowerPoint and Prezi and other tools – but be careful – think, how distracting is some super clever animated image after the first few seconds as you try to pay attention to the speaker?

Moving people, animated graphics, pulsing lines, flashing pictures.

If you have this going on behind you then no-one is listening to

THE PRESENTATION ON PRESENTATIONS

you – they are too distracted – it is bloody annoying, so don't do it.

Ok, use one or two for impact, no problem, but make sure they de-animate after a few seconds so that they do not take away from what you are trying to say.

And when they do stop doing what they do, make sure that visually they still look OK – which leads on to a good key point about presentations, always check a presentation you have built in full 'presentation mode' to make sure it looks as good as you think it does.

Now some thoughts on some of the most common elements of presentational content.

Firstly, the graph.

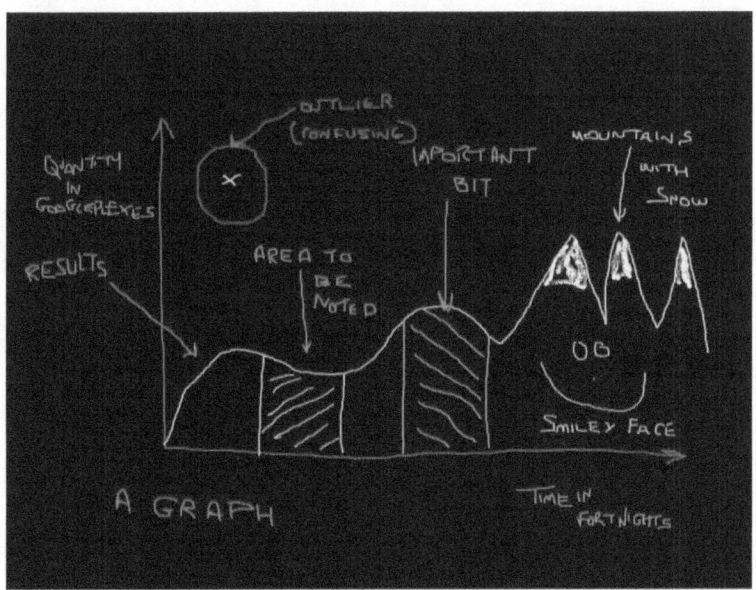

Graphs need to be readable – relevant – meaningful – and as simple as possible. Anything like the above is pointless, people will just stare at it in bewilderment trying to even begin to understand it.

Key points, such as the Bruskin slide earlier: The fear of public speaking, can be isolated for presentation purposes. The Bruskin slides contains many other items of fear but I didn't need to show them all in order to get my message across, and so I selected only what I needed.

If you need to share all the information, then do so in a hand-out.

And then, the data.

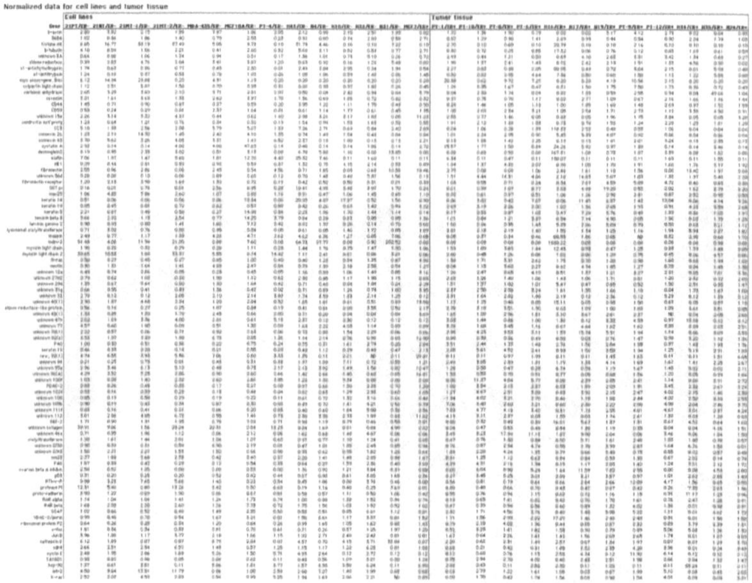
Normalized data for cell lines and tumor tissue
Cell lines
Tumor tissue

You probably can't read this!

If you have to say 'I know you guys at the back can't read this but …' then don't use it.

Hand-outs are a better home for this – or email follows ups –

or web-links etc. – certainly not in your slide deck.

THE PRESENTATION ON PRESENTATIONS

Once more, if there is some valuable point in all this data then draw that out. For example, I could use the above as the backdrop but overlay with the one or two key data points in big bold font. It makes an impact that there is lots of data behind what I am saying, and it makes it clear what my focus is.

13 THE STYLE

Jeff Bezos, of Amazon, told the story behind the new products in images and text at the New York launch for the Kindle Fire and Paperwhite.

THE PRESENTATION ON PRESENTATIONS

The typical PowerPoint slide has forty words. There weren't forty words on ten slides of the Amazon presentation from Jeff.

This is in line with the style of the late Steve Jobs and many other CEOs recently.

This technique is called 'Picture Superiority'.

It simply means that the brain processes information more effectively when the information is presented in pictures and words instead of words alone.

The message here is clear, less (words) is more (impact), more images is better, and to get your message across apply the technique of visual superiority, your audience will love it.

Of course, this goes all the way back to the earlier statement that the slides if you use slides) are for your audience and not for you.

15 THE BODY LANGUAGE

Body language influences your audience, if you are defensive, closed, eyes averted, head down, then the audience will not take to you in a positive way.

Body language also influences yourself. Think about it, you have an important phone call to make, you know that if you take that call sitting down slumped in your comfy chair then you will sound very differently from if you were standing up, attention focused. The same is true of speaking in front of an audience.

Styles on stage –

- Bad
    - Static
- Single tone
- No eye contact
- Good
    - Variable tone
    - Movement
    - Eye contact
- Good delivers
    - Engagement
    - Interest
    - Belief
    - Action
- Bad just doesn't deliver at all

The equipment you have can also impact or limit your body language style.

When I professionally speak, I don't like the restriction of a cabled microphone, it limits my freedom of movement. I can do it, but I much prefer a lapel or head mic.

And then there is the lectern versus free range dilemma. I like to move amongst the audience, as best I can. Being locked to a lectern is really bad. If you are nervous then your hands grasp the side of the lectern and your will be incapable of letting go until the show is all over. Not good.

There is so much written about body language I don't need to cover it here. Just remember, audiences like eye contact, a lively variable tone, and movement of the body in positive and friendly engagement.

16 THE PRACTICALITIES

Think of the three 'Ps' – Prepare, Present, and Profit

Prepare – the better you prepare the better you will be. Practice alone or with a small group – but practice – record yourself, sound or even video, analyse and improve. The technique that works for me is that I a) build the slides b) create notes c) record myself

THE PRESENTATION ON PRESENTATIONS

'presenting' – this is usually a pretty rough presentation but that is OK at this point, then d) I play the recording over and over again when travelling. It is amazing what sticks in your memory this way, plus you get a feel for the flow of the presentation, the highs, lows, the gaps, the 'disconnects' etc.

Then you can improve and, if you wish, do the whole record and listen thing over again.

Present – now is the time to deliver. All that had work thinking, planning, designing, preparing pays off. You are confident and ready.

Profit – if you have prepared well and you have delivered well then you can profit – not necessarily in financial terms but in achieving what you set out to achieve with the presentation; convince, educate or prove (or entertain).

17 THE RISKS

Don't fool yourself. Things can go wrong, so prepare yourself. De-risk what you can de-risk and be ready for the rest.

Do your risk management – what can go wrong?

And what will you do if it does go wrong? What is your 'plan B'?

- Video – will it work, what if it doesn't play

THE PRESENTATION ON PRESENTATIONS

- Sound – speakers, back up options
- Hand-outs – who is preparing these, how many copies
- Microphone – do you need one, is it working
- PC/Presenter compatibility – right lead
- Laptop failure – backup option
- Time changes – less time, different time, how will you cope
- Non attendees – if important/key people are missing how will you deal with this
- New attendees – surprise attendees, number, influence, how will you manage this
- Leavers – disruption to session, key people limited on time, how will this be managed by you

I have experienced all these and more, and in the end, it is all a matter of prepare for the expected and calmly deal with the unexpected whilst never disengaging with the audience. If you have a problem, then explain what is going on.

THE PRESENTATION ON PRESENTATIONS

18 THE RULES

There are some good presentation rules but (after you have started to gain confidence) try breaking a few:

- Rule 1 – is:
    - 6-6-1
    - 6 Bullets per slide – 6 words per bullet – 1 idea per slide

THE PRESENTATION ON PRESENTATIONS

- Rule 2 – is:
    - Tell 'em – Tell 'em – Tell 'em
    - Start by telling the audience what you are going to cover, make the presentation, then repeat the key points in a summary
- Rule 3 – is:
    - Final slide 'Thank the audience'
    - Wrap it all up with a note of appreciation

Now break them – not all at once but in stage

- Rule 1 – Simplify even more – use less words – use more images (picture superiority remember)
- Rule 2 – Just tell the 'story' through your presentation and don't treat the audience like fools, if you have the 'story' right they will get it without you repeating yourself
- Rule 3 – Well maybe thank them by giving them a great presentation experience – but ask for one action at the end perhaps

19 THE HATES

This could be the largest chapter in the book!

There are so many things that an audience might hate about a presentation or presentation experience. Here are just a few:

- Time delays
- Boring text heavy slides
- The agenda of death – 50 minutes in to a 60-minute

THE PRESENTATION ON PRESENTATIONS

       presentation and on point 3 out of a declared 10 points
- Reading the slides
- Not looking at or engaging with an audience
- When the intro is the full unedited CV/Resume of the speaker
- Monotone delivery

I could go on, but I won't (oh yes, the never-ending presentation – or so it seems – when the speaker 'just needs 5 more minutes).

You know what you hate – and so you know what you like – and so you are an expert in what makes for good presentations.

THE PRESENTATION ON PRESENTATIONS

20 THE SURPRISES

Be prepared for anything....

I was asked to speak at an event in Melbourne some time ago.

As I was planning to be in Australia anyway it was a great opportunity and so I quickly agreed.

The event was an end of year celebration, and the location was the

THE PRESENTATION ON PRESENTATIONS

Melbourne aquarium. It was to be fancy dress, nautical themed, and I was to give a humorous and entertaining presentation.

I gave the location no further thought but assumed there was some sort of conference centre attached to the aquarium. I was wrong. The presentation took place inside the aquarium itself, a very impressive building, with fish tanks (that is an understatement) on all sides and overhead.

And so there I was, on a small box, speaking to an audience of mermaids, sea captains, pirates, and other sea- associated creatures, delivering my very best entertaining and fun presentation, and it was going well. Really well as far as I was concerned because the audience was laughing at everything I said.

In fact it did go well, people liked it a lot, but a great deal of the laughter arose from the sight of a large shark circling my head throughout the presentation – as you can see in the picture above.

A classic moment. And, of course, the inspiration for the cover of this book.

So be prepared for anything. You most likely won't have to deal with sharks but in this life, who knows.

THE PRESENTATION ON PRESENTATIONS

21 THE FEEDBACK

Get feedback

It might hurt but it will make you better!

Alfred Bernhard Nobel was born on October 21, 1833 in Stockholm, Sweden

In 1864, when Alfred was 29, a huge explosion in the family's

THE PRESENTATION ON PRESENTATIONS

Swedish explosives factory killed five people, including Alfred's younger brother Emil. Dramatically affected by the event, Nobel set out to develop a safer explosive.

In 1867, he patented a mixture of nitroglycerin and an absorbent substance, producing what he named "Dynamite."

In 1888, Alfred's brother Ludvig died while in France.

A French newspaper erroneously published Alfred's obituary instead of Ludvig's, and condemned Alfred for his invention of dynamite.

Provoked by the event and disappointed with how he felt he might be remembered, Nobel set aside a bulk of his estate to establish the Nobel Prizes to honour men and women for outstanding achievements in physics, chemistry, medicine and literature, and for working toward peace.

Feedback is pretty important right? So, don't be afraid of it, but remember that you cannot and will not please all the people all the time so take a lot of feedback to get a balanced perspective.

22 THE FINAL TIPS

Tip: If you are worried about keeping track of time, then a presenter's 'clicker' can be really useful – especially for new presentations of unproven material. There are many models that incorporate a timer that you can set and that vibrates gently when you have so many minutes left, as well as display the time countdown. If not then make sure you have a clock (even your mobile phone) on display.

Tip: Whilst talking mobile phones – switch it to silent. It is so embarrassing when it is your phone that rings during your own presentation.

Tip: Check your spelling on slides, it is amazing how many errors go up on the big screen and it distracts the audience.

Tip: In the same manner check any tables, numbers, and calculations you display as there will always be at least one person who will pick up on the slightest error and delightedly point it out to you.

Tip: Font size and colour are important. Make it big enough to be seen clearly at the back of the room, and even font size 80 won't be clear if you choose pale green on a yellow background.

THE PRESENTATION ON PRESENTATIONS

Tip: If you are using a presentation tool make sure you review it in full display mode. And then review it again in the actual room, with the actual projector and screen, before you are 'live', it is amazing that what looked great on your high definition widescreen monitor looks less than great on a big screen with a dodgy old projector. Give yourself time to adjust.

Tip: Simon Sinek says you should never talk as you walk out on stage or in front of an audience. 'A lot of people start talking right away, and it's out of nerves,' Sinek says. 'That communicates a little bit of insecurity and fear.' – Simon should know with over 20 million TED views. So, calm yourself and impress, or at least reassure, your audience with your confidence.

Tip: Go watch Simon Sinek on TED, and learn.

Tip: Dress to impress versus being comfortable – always a dilemma, but you know the expectation of dress code for any event therefore just consider if you are 'good to go' in your usual dress standard or is it perhaps worth upping your game just a little if this

THE PRESENTATION ON PRESENTATIONS

is a really important presentation.

Tip: Smile – an audience loves a happy person standing up in front of them and a smile and personable nature will win any audience over, even if you do make a few errors.

Tip: Being passionate can also carry the day. If you believe strongly in something, and don't come across as single minded and lecturing, then the audience will catch some of that passion.

Tip: As for those errors, well you know, it may well only be you who notices them so really don't panic, if it is just minor blip then move on as if nothing happened, if it is a bigger error then acknowledge it, address it, and then move on.

Tip: Make it personal, adding even one simple anecdote can demonstrate to your audience that you are an interesting person and allows them to connect with you so much better. Stories are very powerful presentation devices because of this, with the added advantage that you know these stories well and therefore little preparation is required for that part of the presentation.

Tip: Pause. If you pause for 3 seconds then the audience tends to think you have forgotten something but if you pause for 10 seconds this is not the case. You can do this to make a point, get the audience to think and this also works if you feel you have lost key members of the audience. If you stop talking then pretty much everyone will notice this and stop doing what they are doing and look at you.

Warning – 10 seconds of silence on a stage is a long time but it is a good technique to use very occasionally.

Tip: If someone asks a question and you are using a microphone always repeat the question for the sake of the rest of the audience as they most probably didn't hear he question and for you to go straight in to an answer can be confusing.

THE PRESENTATION ON PRESENTATIONS

Tip: And finally, KISS – Keep it simple stupid – I know, you aren't stupid but if you cram so much in to your presentation that it is fairly bursting at the seams and you feel you just have to cover absolutely everything in your allotted time then it will be feel rushed, you will lose your audience and you will be stressed. Breathe, speak calmly and clearly and win that audience over.

THE PRESENTATION ON PRESENTATIONS

23 THE STORIES FROM THE STAGE

The hot water story

Staying hydrated is very important when speaking.

Always make sure you have a drink (of water) to hand to sip during your presentation. Talking is a very drying experience in that sense.

And taking a sip is also a great chance to catch your breath, have a think, regroup and move on.

One event I requested some water, as there was none, and sure enough a glass of clear fresh water appeared for me.

This was a small event with the projector on a table, laptop on one side and some space on the other, where the water was duly placed for me.

15 minutes into presentation it was time for a drink and yeuk! I got a mouthful of almost hot water since the glass had be placed in the direct blast of the projectors cooling fan, and it was an

THE PRESENTATION ON PRESENTATIONS

> old style projector so it certainly produced some heat.

Moral: Make sure you have water and make sure it doesn't try and boil itself during the talk, it won't be a pleasurable experience.

The biscuit story

> My plane was late, and I was due to speak at an evening event in Ireland.
>
> Not only was my plane late there was actually no food on the flight, but I thought, not to worry, there will be food at the event itself. I will land, grab a taxi, arrive in time for a quick sandwich and drink and do what I try to do best for an attentive audience.
>
> When I eventually arrived at the venue there was only time for a quick coffee and a sample of the only food left. A delicious digestive biscuit.
>
> The outcome of which was that I walked up to the front of the room and began choking, which resulted in a ten minute delay to the start of the presentation whilst I was given a drink of water and recovered to a point where I could actually string a sentence together.

Moral: Better to not eat than try and eat a biscuit before a presentation. Carry a snack with you, just in case.

The one projector story

> On a trip a long way from my home I arrived at an impressive venue. A football stadium.
>
> I was guided into the room where we were planning to have the presentation and I powered up my laptop, checked the connection to the projector. I then walked the

THE PRESENTATION ON PRESENTATIONS

> room as I normally do to assess visual connection for the audience members and my limits of mobility, and I decided all was good.
>
> Just before people walked into the room, they were outside drinking coffee and talking, I powered up the projector again but this time is started to vibrate and, as a result, the screen display was unreadable, and headache inducing.
>
> I called my guide/host over and asked for an alternative projector only to be advised that there wasn't one, it had been sent away for repair.
>
> Realising that use of the projector that we did have was not going to be an option, I switched to a flipchart and black pen and delivered my speech. Since I knew my material well, it all went down in a most acceptable manner and more than one person commented that it made a refreshing change.

Moral: Do your risk management, check, and check again when at the location of the presentation, and always have a backup plan.

The good speaker story

> I was standing ready to present at a local project management meeting, eager and keen to share my experiences but had to wait for the organiser to introduce me.
>
> Now the background story here is that the organiser and their team of volunteers had worked hard to get a schedule of speakers lined up for the rest of the year after a period of no speakers for the local community of project managers.
>
> They were somewhat excited about this achievement.

THE PRESENTATION ON PRESENTATIONS

And so I was introduced as follows 'Before we introduce Peter Taylor to talk to us all about being a Lazy Project Manager I just wanted to let you know that next month we have a really good speaker joining us…'

It wasn't meant that way obviously, but it certainly gave me a challenge to build my confidence up from that point and try and be a 'really good speaker'.

OK, slightly harsh I felt.

Moral: Introductions can often best be delivered by yourself but, as ever, be ready for surprises.

The cut it short story

> I was in New Zealand, miked up and ready for action on stage.
>
> I was the day one closing keynote speaker and I had a pile of books ready to sell and a message of productive laziness to share.
>
> I was ready!
>
> And then the host took me to one side and asked (well it wasn't really and ask, more of a directive) if I could 'cut my session short by 15-20 minutes as they had a last minute surprise celebrity who was speaking after me'.
>
> So now I was not closing keynote, I was being followed by someone the audience knew and presumably loved, a sporting great as it turned out and TV star, and I had to trim my beautifully prepared presentation by 25%.
>
> I did it, because I have built my presentation in modules and was ready for this possibility, and I knew my material well.

THE PRESENTATION ON PRESENTATIONS

> The outcome was I delivered a good presentation (by all accounts) and I met a celebrity.

Moral: Be prepared for the unexpected, and remember, there is always someone 'better' than you waiting in the wings.

The locked out of the building story

> Despite a company organising my flight and hotel and transport to the event location the following morning, I found myself locked out of the event with minutes to go.
>
> The problem was that the event was within a massive shopping and entertainment centre. It was early in the morning well before the main centre opened for business and visitors.
>
> There was a single entrance to allow people in to the event halls and all attendees had clear instructions on where to go and how to get in. I didn't. Neither did my taxi driver, who drove me to the completely opposite end of the building which, to be fair, was the main entrance during opening hours.
>
> Added to this was the inability for me to contact my host through their mobile number as they were busy setting up.
>
> The good news was I did get in on time, thanks to a security guard and some crazy miming (due to language barriers).

Moral: Even when you are in the hands of others check things for yourself, assuming that you might have to get to a location on your own.

The flight cancelled story

> During volcanic times in Iceland (a place, as I think I may

THE PRESENTATION ON PRESENTATIONS

have mentioned, I have long wished to visit) my flight was cancelled.

I re-planned my presentation in to three short sessions for remote delivery with exercises in between, to be run by the organisers.

It worked!

Moral: There is always another way.

THE PRESENTATION ON PRESENTATIONS

24 THE CRIB NOTES

The following may not mean much to you but these are my crib notes for my 'Presentation of Presentation' talk. You don't have to understand them, that is my job, but you can see how simple they are and yet they are more than enough for me to reference when I need them.

If you do have to check something then it is fine to say so, the audience will accept this as a valid 'I want to get it right for you' scenario.

- PURPOSE – Convince + Educate + Prove + (Occasion – Daughter – wedding story)
- CONTENT – Pet subject versus volunteered – don't deliver 100%
- TIME – Audience calculation – last year 7,000 at 60 minutes – 292 days (almost a year) listening
- Better 30 good minutes than 60 dull minutes – who's complained about finishing early?
- GETTYSBURG ADDRESS – 1863, Edward Everett – 2 hours oration at 13,607 words versus Lincoln 271 words = impact

THE PRESENTATION ON PRESENTATIONS

- STYLE – Jeff Bezos – Kindle Fire and White launch – usual 40 words per slide – here note Picture Superiority
- 3 P's – Prepare – Present – Profit
- RULES – 6:6:1 and Tell 'em and Thank you (no call for action)

THE PRESENTATION ON PRESENTATIONS

25 THE COMMON QUESTIONS

Q: How to keep it fresh and engaging whilst remaining professional?

A: Firstly, know your audience, then test your material out beforehand to get an objective view – use the techniques I have talked about already – but do make sure it is in keeping with the audience's culture. You are looking for the engagement but not the shock factor! One of the real challenges I have faced is when you have to use the same template for a presentation that the last 100 presenters have done and it all looks drab and 'samey' – images can help to freshen this up – video works – or walk away from the slides and use the flipchart/whiteboard to hammer home a key point – audience interaction is always a good one – and humour (appropriate humour) really does settle people.

Q: Having started in 'presentation mode', I have a tendency to relax and slip into 'conversation mode'?

A: That is not necessarily a bad thing – some of the best presenters I have seen I felt were just having a conversation with me – they weren't lecturing me or presenting at me – just remember to keep close to the point and on track as your presentation has a purpose

THE PRESENTATION ON PRESENTATIONS

and a time limit.

Q: Most of my presentations I deliver online therefore I do not see my audience and often do not know how well I captured their attention.

A: Well as soon as you lose visual 'eye' contact with your audience then things get whole lot tougher – but some techniques include:

- Humour
- Images
- Pre-engagement through the Survey
- Post-engagement with the Slides and booklet
- You can also ask remote attendees to host a slot of the presentation, or be ready to manage the Q&A session, anything to keep them connected
- You can get local representatives to host a post presentation review for feedback to you
- Rotate the meeting write up around the attendees
- Nancy Duarte – check her out – says 'What's worse than sitting through a really bad presentation? Sitting through a bad one delivered remotely!'
- You need to make the presentation as 'real' as
- possible:
- Stand up to speak – energises your voice (they
- can't see you but they can at least hear you)
- Break the presentation in to smaller consumable interesting pieces with calls to action or calls for thought in between
- You have to make it attractive – you have to
- 'beat the email' attraction
- And make sure you start on time (and this means early for you to make sure there are no technical issues) and you end on time – respect the audience
- And set rules for all – no distractions – sounds –
- calls etc.

THE PRESENTATION ON PRESENTATIONS

Q: How do you deliver a confident sounding concise presentation?

A: Practice – and understanding as much as you can about your audience, basically everything that is in this book

Q: Where can I get free images with high quality resolution pictures for my presentations?

A: The web does have a lot of free resources – and some of pretty high quality – others you can use with an appropriate 'sourced from' statement – does your company have free repository you can use, marketing often do for example – and actually high quality images don't need to be expensive. I use PresenterMedia.com a lot and buy 'x' days access and download a whole bunch of images, templates etc. ready for later use. You could even take you own images – this can be fun to do – and engage with your team before the presentation itself.

Q: How can I learn about my different audiences? For instance, the USA audience is different than the Latin American audience?

A: Not so easy – apart from experience or taking advice from a 'local' – but in the end, all audiences, warm to an honest delivery of a presentation.

Q: Keeping the structure and the presentation path is my biggest challenge. Often, I think a free form presentation is my favourite but still need keep on (prepared) track / structure.

A: Again I go back to practice – if you know your material, and I always use PowerPoint to build my presentations, even if I don't use it to deliver the actual presentation, then you will be better in control even if you free form. You can set simple time targets, one or two that you know you should be at this point at this time in to the presentation – it helps you adjust your pace or re-align yourself to your planned presentation.

THE PRESENTATION ON PRESENTATIONS

Q: How to coach other people on presentation skills without being too directive in what the presentation style should be?

A: Put them on my workshop - only joking – I think you can refer them to watch good presenters (TED) – you can showcase good presentations yourself – get them to self-analyse what their strengths and weaknesses are with regards to presentation skills – get them to a point where they are asking for help/coaching

Q: What is the best way to interact with audience when presenting to a smaller group, where there is on-going Q&A and discussion?

A: You want to present in an intimate way – maybe start with a couple of slides or flipchart and then join the small group, you will become uncomfortable formally presenting to a small group and they will feel uncomfortable as well i.e. no safety in numbers – sit down – become one of them – get one of them to takes notes, list issues/actions on the flipchart – ask their opinions etc.

26 THE FINAL ADVICE

You can also go for the paper bag over your head option, no-one will know it's you!

Good luck – let me know if I can help you and your team...

THE PRESENTATION ON PRESENTATIONS

- Presentation on Presentation
- Presentation Skills Workshop
- Presentation Coaching
- Presenting

All the above can be delivered physically/face to face or remotely.

THE PRESENTATION ON PRESENTATIONS

27 THE INSPIRATIONAL QUOTES

Some inspiration on public speaking to help you on your way:

- You can speak well if your tongue can deliver the message of your heart. John Ford
- Be still when you have nothing to say; when genuine passion moves you, say what you've got to say, and say it hot D. H. Lawrence
- Let thy speech be better than silence or be silent. Dionysius Of Halicarnassus
- If you can't write your message in a sentence, you can't say it in an hour. Dianna Booher
- It usually takes me more than three weeks to prepare a good impromptu speech. Mark Twain
- The success of your presentation will be judged not by the knowledge you send but by what the listener receives. Lilly Walters
- If you don't know what you want to achieve in your presentation your audience never will. Harvey Diamond
- No one ever complains about a speech being too short! Ira Hayes
- The most precious things in speech are the pauses. Sir Ralph Richardson
- Speech is power: speech is to persuade, to convert, to

THE PRESENTATION ON PRESENTATIONS

compel. Ralph Waldo Emerson"
- They may forget what you said, but they will never forget how you made them feel. Carl W. Buechner
- Be sincere; be brief; be seated. Franklin D. Roosevelt

THE PRESENTATION ON PRESENTATIONS

28 THE PRESENTATION SKILLS PROGRAM

Based on my experience in travelling the world and speaking to over 60,000 people, I have developed my own 'Presentation Skills' training to help others achieve more through their own presentations at work and beyond.

This one-day workshop takes you on a journey of understanding as to what makes a good presentation and how you can improve your own style and skills with simple steps.

> 'Peter is a powerful, passionate and persuasive speaker'

> 'If you are looking for a terrific presenter for your event, I highly recommend Peter'

> 'Peter's inspiring style and humour made him one of the top contributors to the event'

Who should attend?

Anybody who just wants to 'present' in more confident and effective way.

THE PRESENTATION ON PRESENTATIONS

Benefits

At the conclusion of this course, students will be able to:

- Understand what makes for a good presentation
- Consider how their audience will react and what they are thinking
- Appreciate the four forms of 'presenting' purpose
- De-risk that next presentation
- Manage time, content, tools and actions
- Receive coaching to prepare for or to review their next presentation

Time	Topic
9:00 -10:00	Introductions Get to know each other presentations
10:00 -11:00	The 'Presentation on Presentations' Better presentational skills delivered using the art of presentation
11:00 – 11:30	Coffee
11:30 – 12:15	Discussion of issues, concerns, challenges etc with regards to presenting Utilises the pre-workshop survey
12:15 – 13:00	The journey of a Presentation From idea to delivery to achievement
13:00 – 14:00	Lunch
13:30 – 16:00	Development of presentations with structured guidance Review, improvements, enhancements Re-Present (Coffee break to be taken during this session)
16:00 – 16:45	Lessons learned – next steps
16:45 – 17:00	Close Review and Feedback
Post-workshop	Virtual coaching (1 hour per student) prior or post presentation

THE PRESENTATION ON PRESENTATIONS

29 THE PUBLIC SPEAKER

With over 380 presentations around the world in over 25 countries Peter has been described as 'perhaps the most entertaining and inspiring speaker in the project management world today'.

He also speaks to many other audiences on presentation skills, communication, change and executive leadership.

Contact him today through www.thelazyprojectmanager.com to discuss your next event

www.ingramcontent.com/pod-product-compliance
Lightning Source LLC
Chambersburg PA
CBHW030451220526
45464CB00006B/2490